Legal & Disclaimer

The information contained in this book is not designed to replace or take the place of any form of financial or marital advice. The information in this book has been provided for educational and entertainment purposes only.

The information contained in this book has been compiled from sources deemed reliable, and it is accurate to the best of the Author's knowledge; however, the Author cannot guarantee its accuracy and validity and cannot be held liable for any errors or omissions. Changes are periodically made to this book. Upon using the information contained in this book, you agree to hold harmless the Author from and against any damages, costs, and expenses, including any legal fees potentially resulting from the application of any of the information provided by this guide. This disclaimer applies to any damages or injury caused by the use and application, whether directly or indirectly, of any advice or information presented, whether for breach of contract, tort, negligence, personal injury, criminal intent, or under any other cause of action.

You agree to accept all risks of using the information presented inside this book.

Contents

Introduction

Why Planning Financials Together is Important?

Before your wedding, I am sure you talked quite a lot regarding money while planning your wedding. These included the decision on how much you are willing to spend on the ceremony, on the reception, and where you could go and how much to pay for your honeymoon. Did you have difficulty discussing who pays for what?

After you have tied the knot, have you ever tried to talk about how you are going to handle other financial decisions?

"For better or for worse; for richer or for poorer." This is what you and your partner have promised when you committed yourselves into marriage. But is it really so easy to survive "for richer or for poorer"? Consider the statistics below.

1. The average couple have arguments with reference to money for about **three** times a month.
2. According to a conducted survey, **a quarter** of couples admit that money is the most common reason for their fights.
3. A recent study at Utah State University found that couples that frequently fight over finances increases their likelihood to get divorced, especially if the fight starts occurring several times a week, or almost every day.

4. About **30%** of couples who disagree about finances eventually get divorced.

Many couples do not have much knowledge or experience in handling money, and may have poor money management skills. Others just do not really think about monetary fusion and they do not even put effort to communicate about such matter. They either continue to manage their own money individually, or one party would take on responsibility for all the financial planning while the other party rely completely on him/her for it. Everything may go well for a while, until you start having to confront your first few disagreements about money. Considering the statistics above, that could be a risky approach if you do not deal with it properly.

Why this Book?

If you want to make the most of both your money **together**, then planning and investing together with your spouse is the smart strategy. This way, you can really optimize your investment and expense for the family together. For example, you do not need to pay separately for two subscriptions that are similar. You do not need to take up two separate insurance policies that over-cover both you and your spouse. By pooling your savings together, you may qualify for a different class of investment that brings you higher return.

However, you must understand that if you and your partner do not come to an agreement on the same goals and the methods of investing, then you are up for a financial – and relationship – disaster once you decide to pool your money. Imagine having two chefs in a kitchen who do not agree on how things should work, it would be a big problem! And the same applies for your investments as well.

Thus, to avoid getting into conflicts regarding financial matters, it is advisable that you have some open conversation and planning with your partner on how to approach this topic. The purpose of this book is to guide you on how to approach financial planning with your spouse, so that you can come up with a plan that enables both of you to **enjoy** the **wealth creation journey** together. The two key points here are

1. **Wealth Creation** – so that you eventually create enough wealth to pursue your dreams, goals, interests etc that money can buy

2. **Enjoy the Journey** - Creating wealth will not happen overnight, and it is a long journey. The important point is to

make sure that you are enjoying the journey together. Ie. You get to enjoy each other's loving company, and you do not get into frequent fights due to financial disagreements, fights that slowly chew away the loving and caring relationship you have for each other until they eventually destroy your marriage.

My biggest hope for you is to help you preserve the love you have for your spouse as you proceed to create wealth together. Happy reading!

Chapter 1 - Expect to Fight Over Money

Financial Fights are Part of Your Marriage Package

Before the wedding bells, when you were just living alone, you probably already had some plans in mind. Being independent with the money you were earning, you were able to come up with goals you want to achieve. You bought things that appealed to you, and invested in things that made sense to you. But along the way, you met someone who eventually turned out to be your life partner. As you got to know this someone, you both decided you want to be with each other for the rest of your life. So you decided to tie the knot. However, just because you are compatible with each other, it does not mean that you agree on all matters every single time. One issue in which you will most often argue a lot about is money.

All healthy marriages have disputes about money. Once you say "I do", you should expect to fight about finances because it is part of the whole marriage package. Even though you and your partner have never argue and feels like you would not argue about money matters, down the road, you will likely face challenges and differences in opinion. Planning separately is easy, whereas planning together is so much more difficult. But being married means doing most things together, and this includes planning financially. However, it is because of this whole financial planning affair that most couples battle against each other.

Why Couples Fight About Money?

There are three common reasons why couples fight about money.

1. The most common reason is when **one of you earns more than the other**. Although this is a common scenario in a household, what really causes fury between you and your spouse is when the secondary earner consistently spend a bigger portion of the money than they make. This resentment may creep in over time. The one who earns more between the two of you may one day call this out in an outburst. He/she will use the other's spending habits as a grenade in a fit of the moment even though he may not have any planned intention to hurt the other party. But bringing this up on the table will inevitably hurt the other party, and this would start planting the seed for financial disagreements. This could be

worse when only one of you earns income in your household, making the other completely dependent on him/her.

2. The second reason is due to both of you **having different objectives**. For example, you are the more risk-averse between the two of you so you want to set your money aside into your retirement fund, while your partner is more consumption-oriented and wants to buy a new car. You then argue with your partner, "Is it really necessary to have a car or should you just put your money away in your 401(k)?" Bringing this up because of having different goals will lead into a lengthy discussion between you and your partner, and if not handled well, could have bad consequences.

3. The third reason is due to **different personalities and value system**. One of you may be considered as the "fun" parent, while the other one would be considered as the "pragmatic" one. How you choose to spend your money while the kids are growing up can be a point of argument. The fun parent would be inclined to spend easily on the kids so that they can have a blissful childhood. The pragmatic parent on the other hand would think that the family should stash away their limited funds to buy books and clothes instead of spending it on movies or amusement parks. Although both of you are right, who should prevail?

Besides the above three, there could be many other reasons. Understanding the reasons for your arguments may provide both of you better insights on how to handle them. Very often, emotions also take part in the arguments. When couples fight, it is usually not about the math, but rather more on what the money means to him or her.

If you fail to identify and address the emotions, but instead try to approach from a purely logical and reasonable angle, it could be a waste of time and energy. Take for example, buying a gift. From a logic perspective, it may not make sense to buy an expensive gift for your partner, and you both could be financially better off saving these money for creating wealth together. But, if the other party starts to feel not loved because of this, then emotions can get in the way.

Handling Financial Disagreements

After learning the reasons for having fights about money, it is important that you come up with an agreement about how to handle disagreements and fights. The best way is to be able to **"Disagree agreeably"**, as experts say. In this case, you recognize differences in each other's views and acknowledge them even if you do not agree with them. Then you seek to find a win-win solution, or at least a compromise, that respects each other's point of views.

But sometimes, this can be easier said than done, especially when one of you brings up an offensive issue without any warning.

For example. "We never have enough money." or "You spent how much on what?"

Then before you realized it, all of a sudden, the fighting bell has rung, and both of you are already exchanging verbal punches. That is why it is important that you talk about and agree on rules for your arguments if they occur, and commit to honor the rules. This is much like boxers being briefed before the match on the rules of the fight, - not to score on the eye, bite, or hit below the belt etc.

It is normal to have a battle about money once you are married, but it is how you fight that is important. If you do not want a bad fight with your spouse that starts eating away your relationship and your marriage, you must play by the rules and come up together with some resolution that both can support.

When disagreements start aggravating into fights, one key strategy to resolve the problem is to calm down. Agree with your spouse that it is okay to disagree for now and then take a break. Give yourselves some space and time to cool your heads before coming to the same topic again. Meanwhile, remind yourself how much you love your partner and that you want him or her to be happy while on the same journey towards wealth creation with you. Also try to assess what you can do to help your partner attain what he or she wants. Ideally you can do this without compromising what you yourself want, but if not, try to find some creative ways to compromise something which you can live with in order for your spouse to achieve his/her objectives. It is easier to find common grounds with your spouse this way. Of course, it helps a lot if your partner can reciprocate this approach, but do not insist and carry this expectation.

Dealing with issues over money in your marriage is normal, and it does not mean that there is something wrong with your relationship. The key to making your marriage work is to ride the ups and downs of your liabilities, wages, and household bills while not losing sight of the big picture of enjoying each other's company and creating wealth together.

Chapter 2 - How to Stop Fighting and Create Wealth Together

Everyone have Different Money Personality

As mentioned in previous chapter, one of the reasons many couples fight over money is because they have different personalities. These include their ideas, opinions, aspirations, and values which were influenced by their environment while growing up. With too much arguments, a sweet marriage can start to break down over time and that would be such a pity.

To avoid this, you have to make sure that you are on the same financial page as a couple. Learn what you and your partner think about money and how you deal with it. Are you good at handling it or are you bad with it? Are you or your spouse a big spender or spends money carelessly? Does he or she understand the means of taking care of your household finances? If one or both of you have negative behaviors with regards to money, it will certainly stop you from creating wealth in the long run and hold you trapped in bad financial habits. This will put a limit on your capacity of managing your wealth. To get that fixed, the best tip for married couples like you is to learn about each other's money personalities.

Your money personalities are usually developed from your childhood, when you were taught by your parents what to do with the money they gave you. They might have given you a piggy bank where you can put a dollar a week, and you need to save up enough money before you can buy the things you want. Practicing a saving habit like this will most probably lead you to be good at saving as you get older. Conversely, if you had never need to worry about money when growing up, and your parents are always able to buy anything you want for you, you are unlikely to be a saver, and will continue to spend money easily in your adult life and even after marriage.

Exploit Each Other's Money Personality

Your money personalities may complement each other. If you are good at balancing checkbooks and your spouse is good at shopping for good deals, then make use of both your expertise. Be the financial investor of the family, while letting your partner be the penny pincher to help save up even more money.

Once you are done learning about each other's money personalities, it is important for both of you as a married couple to work with your strengths. Pay attention to what comes naturally from both of you and make use of them efficiently by agreeing how to allocate financial tasks between you and your spouse.

If need be, seeking external help is also a good option. For example, if neither of you are knowledgeable or experienced when it comes to managing finances, then you might want to consider asking help from a financial adviser. You can get advices on how to save, invest, and grow your money from these professionals. Chapter 4 will give you some basic education to get both of you started with some basics.

Seek First to Understand, Then be Understood

When working through financial arrangements, it is also essential to respect each other's opinions and try to understand each other's position. When one of you is explaining about why it is important to spend so much on something, let him or her finish what he or she has to say. Do not cut him or her off. Otherwise, you should not expect that you will be able to finish your own thoughts at some point in the conversation as well. No matter what personality you and your spouse have towards money, try to understand fully, and then accept the way things are.

There may be differences that you do not like but if you really love your partner, then you should not force him or her to change so that he or she can be more like you. But that does not also mean that you should blindly accept everything that you do not like. For example, your wife wants an expensive yearly family vacation that you think you could not afford. Or perhaps your husband has an obsession with Star Wars such that he collects every movie, toy, and any forms of merchandise he finds available. It would be perfectly reasonable if you try to come up with a compromise where less money should go towards the vacation your wife wants, or the Star Wars merchandise your husband loves. However, if you tell your spouse that it is not important to have a family vacation or that spending on Star Wars merchandise is a stupid thing to do, then you are being unreasonable.

It is important not to neglect personal preference too. If your partner talks about a personal preference and you try to beat it out of him or her every time, then wake up! It is you who lacks communication skills. Once you keep on doing this, you are building up for a disaster. If you feel like the only way to survive is getting your partner to change and be more like you, you are only belittling him or her. If you can accept the difference between you and your partner's spending habits, then you are in a much better position to work and solve the problems together. Both of you should start from the point of really trying to uncover and understand the other party's points of view, personalities, and preference. and then at the same time, make the other party understand your own. Do this calmly and maintain respect and openness by listening intently, and you would be able to work out a common solution that both can accept.

The whole process is definitely easier to describe than to actually do it. At some times, you may even wonder... If you are married to someone who is so different from you when it comes to finances, wouldn't it have been better if you did not marry at all? Quickly dispel this thought and recognize that this is not necessarily true. Even if you and your partner are different, you may potentially complement each other. It could even be more damaging when a couple is like-minded. For example, if both of you are spenders, then nobody is going to worry about overspending and saving. And if both of you are savers, then nobody is going to get on a vacation. Would that be gratifying in the long run?

The important thing is to recognize that your partner would have different money personalities and preferences. We just need to be open to explore to understand each other, and then learn to respect each other's differences, and work out an optimal plan together. Remember the maxim - *"Seek first to understand, then be understood"*.

By doing this, we may realized that we could exploit each other's strengths to achieve better outcomes together and speed up our wealth creation process. The earlier we do this, the better, before all the disagreements starts ending up into ugly fights, and when emotional stakes are high, it becomes more difficult to work out a compromise.

Our book talks about creating wealth together. You can only achieve this if you work together. You can't achieve this if you keep spending your time fighting each other, and even if you finally managed to accumulate money, your relationship could end up broken and you would not enjoy the fruits of this success together, and that would be such a pity. Thus this chapter lays the foundation for you to sort out the differences and find common grounds to move forward together.

Chapter 3 - Establish a Common Plan and Budget

Why You Need to Create a Common Plan?

After you have sort out your differences and agreed on a common approach to create wealth together, you are now ready to embark on the journey together. But before you begin your journey, you need to know where you want to go. There is a saying - "*If you know not where you are going, any road is fine.*"

Let's avoid that, and make sure you have a plan together on where you want to land, and then you can make plans to go there together. Having a plan which both of you share will also bond both of you with a shared vision of your future together. With this plan that you share together, it becomes the compass for many decisions during your journey, and when the road gets rough, the plan will be there to guide you. It will be there to remind you of your common dreams and goals, as well as what is important in both your life, and guide your key financial decisions along the way.

Begin with the Endpoint in Mind

What's in the plan? First and foremost, it must have an endpoint where both of you want to reach together. You need to discuss and set this together, and it differs for every couple. A common desired endpoint for many couples may be the following, but you should discuss and set your own one.

> *"Both of you are financially independent by age of say 60 years old, and need not be worried about money when both of you are retired at that age. You would already a dream house which both of you shared with your kids, and your kids have already finished college education and already working and financially able to take care of themselves. Both of you have enough money to go for vacation together, and you spend your remaining years traveling to different places, continuing to enjoy the loving company of your spouse for the remainder of your life."*

In setting you desired endpoint, it is also important to be realistic. Some may think retiring at 60 is way too slow, and they would want to retire by 40 instead. This is not unachievable for some as it depends on what they have to start with at the beginning of the journey - Maybe a large inheritance would bring forward their plans by many years. But you should exercise caution not to set overly ambitious goals. If the goals are too ambitious, along the way you would realized that you are unable to reach that goal. Unless you are able to re-plan your goals, otherwise the goal may just fall apart, and along with that, possibly your common dreams together. It is definitely wiser to set goals that are not too ambitious so that your expectations are low, but while you continue to work hard, and if you manage to over-deliver on that expectations, then both of you can get to be pleasantly surprised along the way.

Catering for Various Scenarios Along the Way

After your have endpoint set, you know which direction you are generally headed. But your life together is going to be a long journey, and there will be many obstacles along the way. Every time you hit an obstacle, it is better that you already have a planned-out response to it and can therefore react or re-plan accordingly in a calm manner. Along the way, you would also be hitting some milestones, and that should provide a reality check for you to see if you are still on track, and then allow you to assess if your plans are still feasible, and whether you need to re-plan your routes.

The following section discusses common scenarios that you would face and for which you need to be prepared for.

Handling Big Purchase

Buying any big ticket items will cause a big drain in your financial pool, and potentially set your plan back a bit. If not handled properly, this has great potential to result in big fights or major disappointments for one or both party.

You need to find a common ground when it comes to such big purchases. These can be in forms of houses, cars, or any major investments. When it comes to getting these big ticket items, make sure that you and your partner do not only discuss the practical details on the purchases, but also the emotional facets associated with them. You need to spend time to fully understand each other's money personalities, value system, opinions, preferences etc. Spend time to fully understand what the item means to each other, and make sure to have open honest discussions. Learn to voice out your feelings about big purchases with composure and rationality, and not let your anxiety to get what you want get ahead of the discussion. If necessary, one or both party may need to take turns to make compromise and concessions in order to move the discussion forward.

Spending on Special Occasions

Special occasions may be in the nature of anniversaries, birthdays, or any other celebrations - your in-law's big days may sometimes need to be accounted too. They are special days and should not passed unnoticed, like any other days. They are days which both of you can look forward to enjoy yourself, and this is also part of having fun together along your lifelong journey together. There are divorce cases where one party feels that the other party does not love her enough to spend enough on her big days. Ouch...

Therefore it is advisable to pre-plan all your "special days" and allocate a budget to spend on each of these days. But, if you and your partner have different thoughts on how much is a "reasonable" amount of money to be spent on each special occasions, then this could lead to a arguments and disappointments too. Again you need to find ways so that you can meet halfway with your partner. When you lined up all these special days, and see the total amount you would be spending for each of them, you would know if they are within your means - considering your income, other expenses, and your target saving every month etc. If they are not, you would need to make some adjustments together to the amount allocated to each occasion. This may involve prioritizing one occasion over another to spend more money, and this can be a source of frequent disagreements too. So tread carefully here.

Do remember, you can also opt for cheaper ways to celebrate some special occasions, like having a home-cooked dinner or watching your favorite movies while cuddling on the couch, versus expensive dinner at high-class restaurant to show your affection for the other party.

Spending on Weekend Getaways, Vacations and Family Holidays

Similar to special occasions, your marriage together will be so monotonous without some of these special moments together where you can spend time away for a break from daily routines. These are the periods where you can inject some fun along the way in your lifelong journey together, and remind yourself why you get married in the first place - to be together and to have fun together.

Differences on how you dish out your funds for time off work, what to do, and how much to spend on trips could turn a dream vacation into a nightmare. To avoid negative attitudes from going off, realistically plan your itinerary ahead of time, such as deciding whether you are flying economy or first class, staying at a hotel or a friend's house, etc. Work out a schedule on how frequent you want to go for these, how much you can afford to spend etc.

Spending on Kids

It may not be easy to control when they would come to your family, but when they do, though they bring both of you a lot of joy, they would be another big drain on your financials which you need to be prepared for. Not only will you need to incur a one-time expense for each kid, your monthly expenses will go up, and thus could affect the amount you can save, and thus slow you down in your wealth creation process. Therefore, you need to remake a budget and make changes to your plan by adjusting your spending for other items accordingly. Example, maybe spending less on holidays while setting aside some extra money for their college educations etc.

As the kids are growing up, the amount needed to spend on them can vary widely. You can choose to indulge them with expensive toys and gadgets and bring them to expensive places together so that the family can always have a good time, or choose to give them only the basics and make them save up or even work for their own toys so that they will learn the importance of money management early in their childhood. It is important that you align this approach early too, because if you have different ideas on this, and choose to act differently using your common funds, not only are you sending inconsistent message to your kids, sooner or later, you would end up in disagreements too.

Handling Promotions, Bonus, Wage Increases and other Windfalls

These are supposed to be positive things that add more spending power and bring you a step nearer to wealth creation. But, if not handled properly, can again lead to disagreements and fights on how to use this money and where to allocate the extra money. Should you save or should you spend it? If spend, on where?

To prevent this, make sure that you two talk about decisions on how you would deal with such scenarios. Keep in mind that both of you may have different views on how to handle this money, so discussing and agreeing is important.

Handling Salary Reductions, Layoffs, and Un-employment

Corporate life nowadays are very unpredictable. It is common to have salary reductions and layoffs when business is not doing well. When you are younger and earning less, you probably can get re-employed relatively fast, but once you reach a certain income level, it can take longer to be re-employed.

When these events happen, they can have big implications to your short term budget, and even longer term plan. They could also affect your self-esteem, confidence levels, and cause emotional disappointments to the affected party. Many times, people avoid talking about this, assuming it would not happen, and when it happened, they again avoid talking about this, and end up feeling very depressed. Guys have more tendency to keep this to themselves and try to find a solution themselves. But this does not always work out, and the stress during this period experienced by him could really spark off a lot of disagreements and fights. Sad to say, many cases of divorces happened during such times of stress and financial difficulties, often with one party wondering why suddenly another party has changed drastically, and is no longer the loving spouse he/she used to be.

Thus, in making your financial plans, recognize that these events can happen, and agree to discuss about it when it happen. Then come up with a response to deal with it together, and be open to adjust your lifestyle whenever such events occur. Do note that there are many people who managed to build huge financial wealth outside corporate jobs, and thus losing a corporate job does not necessarily means an end to financial income. It could even be a blessing in disguise for one of you to start pursuing some of those other revenue possibilities that you were both too busy to pursue when your corporate jobs are tying you down and sucking up all your energy.

If you are open to discussing these items, sometimes you may even recognize the risk before any bad events happen, and start building up a contingency plan to have alternate streams of income outside your corporate job. One alternate stream of income is of course from your investments, where hopefully you build up enough financial wealth such that you do not need to depend on corporate income to sustain yourself, and can live off your dividends and other savings. There are also potentially many other forms of such alternate incomes that are not covered by this book, but you can easily research more of them yourself over time.

Setup a Common Budget and Manage it Together

Once you have set up a common plan by knowing your endpoint, have recognized and planned out appropriate responses to some key scenarios along your journey to reach your endpoint, you should start to setup a common budget, and then manage it together. Having such a budget, and reviewing and managing it regularly together will allow you to track how you are progressing towards your goal, and keep both of you motivated to keep pushing towards your dream point.

Plan out how much money each of you should spend. Have a weekly check in to see if you are doing well. As you review your actual spending against the budget, you may also realized ways to further optimize your budget so that you can allocate more money to savings and investments, while not taking away any fun out of both your lives together. Any extra savings you can put aside each month, if proper invested, will make a big difference in the long run.

Should You Keep Some Money in Separate Accounts?

This is a common question and there is no fixed answers. It would vary widely from couple to couple. If both couples are totally capable of agreeing every time on everything, then this is absolutely the best thing to do with your combined pool of money.

There can be however many cases where this can prove too challenging. Rather than forcing agreements and compromise every single time, one good approach would be to agree to disagree and let each other have some freedom to manage his or her budget separately to do anything that he or she fancy, while not jeopardizing the common plan.

In this case, the approach may be to agree on setting aside a portion of each other's salary and pool them into the common account where both of you manage together. The rest can be retained separately by each other for use on anything each of you fancy, and both of you can spend your own portion on anything without having to consult your partner and your partner should give you the space to do this as well. Then both of you focus on the common account, and managing what you have in there.

The proportion to be set aside for common account would vary from couple to couple, and you as a couple would have to sit down and agree on that together. For higher chance to create wealth together, then the bigger this portion the better. However, if both of you have difficulty agreeing on how to spend this common pool of money all the time, then setting aside the minimum for common management may also be a good idea out of no choice, because at least it would prevent you from having too much disagreements and fights, that ultimately derail your marriage, and the dream to create wealth together.

So in this case, set aside just the amount both of you are comfortable so that it can cover your common agreed expenses, and make sure you still have some budget surplus to invest in something that both of you can agree to.

Chapter 4 - Investment Basics

This chapter aims to give you a short introduction to the basic theories of investing, which is fundamental for wealth creation. If both of you are pretty good at investments, you may skip this section, or skim through quickly. The content alone in this chapter will not be sufficient for your wealth creation journey, and you need to supplement this by a lot of extra readings and research. But the hope here is to get you initiated so that you can go and look out for better ways to invest and build your wealth wisely.

Saving versus Investments

Saving is allocating or setting money aside, little by little, to bring together a lump sum for future consumption. Setting a goal to have money for a holiday, a deposit on a house, or any emergencies that might come up, usually require you to save. Saving often means putting your money into cash, such as in your cookie box, or in a bank. The money is readily available when you want it.

Investing, on the other hand, is setting aside some of your money with the objective of making it grow. It is a sacrifice of current use of money but with the expectation of an increase in the future. It is considered a sacrifice because you are putting in money on investments – such as in buying stocks, property, or shares in a fund – instead of using it for immediate consumption, and the money may not be immediately available when you need them. Meanwhile, it comes with an expectation that you have returns to obtain afterwards, although you do not know how much or when exactly since it is dependent on the movements of the market.

The main differences between saving and investing are the degree of risk and the level of returns. When it comes to saving, there is little or no worries at all that we do not get back our money when we want it, and thus we say it has little to no risks. In investing, putting aside your money may involve risk that you do not get back your invested amount, or at least not when you want it. When you save, you know exactly how much you will get once you decide to withdraw your savings. When you invest, you are usually unsure of the returns you will get. It can be a gain but could also possibly be a loss, depending on how your investment turned out.

Why Should You Invest?

Some people invest for supplemental income. This means getting additional income aside from the income they earn from work. Example if you invest in a stock that pays dividend regularly, then the dividend you get every period is your additional income. If your investment is huge enough, that income is sufficient to cover your expenses and you need not depend on your corporate job to give you the income you need to sustain yourself.

Others invest for appreciation of money. If you only have a small pool of money to start with, investing for supplemental income will not give you much income, unless you grow that pool into a more substantial figure. Thus you need to multiply your pool, and the way to do so is to let it appreciate. For example, Investing something with $10, and after a period of time, you get back $100. If you keep doing this, this pool can grow quite substantial, until a point, it can be put into regular income for you and your spouse to cover your expenses, and allow you to retire and stop working, while still having enough to enjoy life together.

As they say, there are two ways to make money: 1) by working for money, or 2) by having your money work for you. And (2) is what investment is all about.

If you decide to save by putting your money in your closet instead of investing it, you are not letting your money work for you, and you will never have more money than what you already have in that box. By choosing to invest your money wisely, you are letting your money work for you to generate more money.

Types of Investments

There are two main types of investment. The first type is a fixed return investment. This happens when someone borrows money from you for a period of time. When you get back the money you lent, you collect interest. How much interest you gain depends on how risky it is for you to get back your principle and the promised return. With this type of investment, your return and the timing of getting it tend to be more predictable. If the risk is well managed, they are very suitable for providing income supplement as mentioned earlier.

The second type of investment involves capital appreciation with variable return. For example, buying assets such as stocks in a company, or a piece of property. The objective is to hope to buy the asset at a lower price, and when the time is right, sell it for a higher price and pocket the difference. We call it capital appreciation because the capital which you initially used for investment should have appreciated if you invested wisely. The only problem with this type of investment is that the price may not necessarily end up higher than what you paid, and even if it does eventually goes back to the same or higher level, it is hard to predict when this can occur. Thus this type of investment is not suited for regular income, but if invested wisely, can be a good chance to get capital appreciation over time. There are many real examples of people who have invested in a piece of property during economy downturn, and after riding out the downturn, went on to earn multiple times of what they invested.

Risk-Return Trade-off

There is a saying "The greater the risk, the greater is the return." The reverse is most likely true too. There is no free lunch, and every investment carries some degree of risk. In order to compensate you for taking more risk before you can get back your money, you are usually rewarded with a higher return. Conversely, anybody that promised you a high return for your money is likely to incur more risk for you. To think otherwise would be foolish.

If your financial goal are for longer term, you may generate more money by investing it in higher-risk assets such as stocks or bonds. In contrast, if your financial goals are for a short term, investing in less risky investments may be a more appropriate option for you.

Also, different people may have different risk appetite. One may be more willing to risk their money in order to generate higher potential return, while another may be totally unwilling to take much risk, and would be perfectly comfortable if he can generate a very low return with pretty good certainty. The latter person is also known as being more risk-adverse. It is very likely you and your spouse may have very different risk appetite, so you need to recognize this when you do your financial planning.

Power of Compounding

One key element of investing is compound interest. This makes you earn interest on the money you save and on the interest that your money earns. Even a small amount of savings can add up to a big amount of money over time to help you obtain your financial goals.

It has been even said that compound interest is a millionaire's best friend, and the power of compounding is one of the key secret in getting rich slowly.

Let me give you an illustration on how compound interest works. For example, if you were to save $1 every day. That will add up to $365 a year. If you choose to put that amount (principal) into an investment with a 5% annual interest, you get to have $468.67 by the end of five years. If you keep investing that, you will end up getting an amount of $1,635.82 by the end of thirty years. Imagine investing a larger principal with a higher interest, how much profit can you gain in later years? Now that is the power of compounding. We will cover this topic again in later in more details.

Diversification

Investing does not only mean allotting your resources into one single investment. There is a famous saying *"Do not put your eggs in one basket."* This means that you should not invest all of your assets into one single investment. This is because any investment carries some form of risk, and if "the basket is dropped", you will lose all of the money that you have invested.

That is why there is such a thing called diversification. Diversification means distributing your money (or assets) among different investments. You may put some money in various financial assets like stocks, bonds, and mutual funds. You may also diversify further and place investment in another class of assets like land, building, shop-houses or basically anything which are subject to mortgage if purchased via credit.

It is important to diversify your assets to be able to achieve a given level of expected returns (gains) but bearing manageable risks. Diversification helps to reduce the risk of your overall investments (also known as a "portfolio").

In Summary...

Investing is a big topic and would require much more than one simple chapter to cover them. You are advised to research and study more about investments together if you want to create wealth together. If both of you are not born with a silver spoon and have only an average job, the key to creating wealth together is to learn to invest together wisely so as to grow your income through capital appreciation, until it reaches a certain nest egg, where both of you can start drawing a fixed income from it to cover your expenses and support your desired lifestyle.

But as all investment carries some risks, you have to learn to diversify your investments, and also understand the risk return trade-off. As it is likely you and your spouse may have different risk appetite, you also need to agree upfront what risk you both want to accept. Finally, in selecting stocks, mutual funds etc. for investment, it is very important that you spend time studying them, and do not invest blindly without research. If you are unsure or unfamiliar, always seek out professional help.

Chapter 5 - Investing as a Couple

Assess Risk Profiles and Deciding How to Work Together

Now that you already have a basic idea about investing and have learned about how to deal with financial matters with your spouse, let us now focus on investing as a couple. Before going further, try answering a risk profile questionnaire individually and compare your answers afterwards. You can get a copy of the risk profile questionnaire from any financial consultant or financial institution. If you cannot get your hand on one, then you may also download a copy from the resource link I would provide you at the end of this book.

It is important that you understand your partner's background on finance and experiences before you decide on investing together. It is common that one spouse tends to invest heavily whereas the other tends to spend heavily. If not aligned properly upfront, this can be the perfect recipe to put an end to plans or worse – your marriage.

Based on the risk profile questionnaires that you have completed with your spouse, you may find that both of you have different levels of risk aversion. To find a common ground, talk with your spouse about how both of you should handle risks, and as much as possible, get to know about each other's styles and tendencies when it comes to investing. Your discussion should also extend towards the lessons both of you have learned from your parents while growing up and regarding the sources of your wealth as well.

After you have understood each other's views, try to find a solution for you and your spouse to commit to working together. If one of you is more knowledgeable or passionate on a specific kind of investment or perhaps has extra time to keep an eye on the investment, then he or she can take the lead in investing matters. It is important to pre-discuss and determine who will be the one between the two of you who will control the purse string and release funds for investment, as well as who will evaluate the information you acquire concerning investment opportunities so that you do not miss out your chance of gaining more money. They can be the same person, or it can be two different person such that one will evaluate and present the opportunities to the other for additional layer of assessment before releasing funds to invest. Ideally, it would be better if both of you are involved in analyzing opportunities and discussing investments together. This is part of creating wealth together.

Using Financial Educations to Align Both of You

When both of you first come together, you may discover that one is from Mars and the other from Venus when it comes to finance. For example

- The needs of men and women could be very different. Example, women tend to prefer security while men prefers to be successful quickly.
- Your risk profiles are different. Example, one prefers more risky investment for chance to create wealth faster, while the other prefers to go safe and steady.
- Your financial education and backgrounds are different and you have different starting point. One could be much more financially literate and savvy in investment, while the other is completely ignorant.

If the differences are too great, you may find that it is difficult to understand each other and reach common grounds to move forward. Rather than forcing this process and end up with disagreements, or having one party end up dictating all the decisions while the other party passively submits to these decisions, it is highly recommended that both you and your spouse spend time to get educated about financial planning. There are many ways to do this, like getting common books to read, talking to financial planners, attending financial seminars etc.

It is not advisable that one of you will make the decision for the other party, especially when the one who will make the decision does not fully understand the other's goals and aversion towards risk. Although it is quite normal that one party takes control over financial decision-making in the relationship, doing things together will always end up with better results. Investing in some financial education together will bridge the financial gaps between both of you and improve both of your financial understanding.

When both of you have similar financial understandings through the common financial educations you attend together, you will find it much easier to make financial decisions together without much fighting due to differences. The ability to easily make decisions and brainstorm ideas together as a couple without fights not only improve the relationship with each other, but also tend to result in higher quality decisions that both can agree to and commit to execute as well.

Mapping the Investment Strategy

After you understand each other's risk profile, and are both financially educated to the point where you are comfortable to plan together, you can start to work on an effective investment strategy together.

Step 1 - Set Investment Objectives

Begin by setting some investment objectives. Example,

- To purchase a dream home or a second home for investment purpose.
- To finance a child's education.
- To set up a business to pursue your dream or interest
- To retire by certain age.

After setting up these objectives, estimate the needed amount of money by the time these objectives are needed.

Step 2 - Establish Monthly Budget

Consider the income that both of you are getting today, minus away all the expenses that you will need throughout the month. This will give you a net figure which you can put into savings or investment every month. If you want to create wealth faster, then this number needs to be larger. If the number turns out to be negative, you are spending beyond your means and need to figure out ways to cut back your expenses.

When setting budget, remember to include everything that you would need to spend money on. Example, gifts, toys and gadgets that you would like to buy for you or your spouse every once in a while, etc. If you end up spending less than what you budget, consider that a bonus which you can add to your investment or saving faster.

If you are maintaining separate accounts, then plan the budget for the common account. This account will be funded by an agreed proportion of your individual incomes minus away the common expenses. Again, it should be positive, and the higher the surplus number, the faster the wealth creating process.

Step 3 - Work out the Maths

This is the hardest part, and also where reality sets in, and you may need to repeatedly go back and make changes to what you have drafted in Step 1 (Your Objectives) and Step 2 (Your Budget).

Your budget determines what you can save every month, which you can put into savings or investments. You need to calculate if the savings every month, through proper investments, can help you achieve your various objectives. To do this, consider the interest rates or the rate of returns you will likely be able to get, and whether after factoring them, it can help you achieve your goals. Some financial modeling may be needed here, and if you are not too sure how to do this, you should consider getting help from financial planners.

After some calculation, you may likely find that you are unlikely to meet your goals with just savings, and even with investments that provide reasonable returns. This would mean you need to make some adjustments to your plans. Example,

- Your objectives may need to be prioritized so that the more important ones get achieve first, and the rest you will try on a best effort basis.
- You may need to downgrade some of your investment objectives. Eg. If you budget a million for your dream house, maybe you may downgrade to half a million instead for a smaller house.

- You may adjust your budget plans to increase the net amount you can save after deducting the expenses. As mentioned, the more you can save, through the power of compounding, the more substantial you can grow your wealth, and thus more likely to achieve your goals.

While this process is frustrating, and sometimes very de-motivating, because you need to keep lowering your expectations for your dream, and keep increasing the savings (which means you cannot indulge yourself so much now), it will serve to make both of you much more aware of what you need to do in order to leave enough money to pursue all the things that really matters to both of you. It is much better to have all these disappointments now, and keep adjusting your plans, than to have these disappointments when you are both 10 to 20 years older. At that age, both your options for growing your wealth becomes significantly constrained because you do not have enough time to save up for what you need even though you may be extremely willing. So the earlier you start to recognize what you need to do in order to achieve your goals, the higher the chance you can attain them. This whole concept is explained more clearly in later chapter.

Besides controlling costs to achieve your budget savings, it is important to recognize that you can work on income too. Example, find additional source of income for both you and your spouse is one possibility (but not in the scope of this book). As both of you are young, there is always possibility of wage increase over time, or perhaps you will get promoted along the way, and thus your income can be significantly expanded with these promotions. As long as you do not spend all the extra income that you get, you will have the opportunity to put more money into savings, and thus speed up the wealth creation process, and possibility help you achieve some of your original goals too.

Consulting Financial Planners

To help you reach your goals, you might want to consider working with a professional financial planner to help you plan out an investment and asset allocation strategy. Financial planners can help you by giving you advice on the best ways to save, invest, and grow your money. They can assist you in dealing with a particular financial goal – such as buying a house – or providing you with an assessment of your money and advise you on the various assets available and most suitable for your investment. Look for a certified financial planner (CFP) to give you advice on finances. CFPs are licensed and regulated. Furthermore, they take compulsory classes on different aspects of financial planning, so you are sure that your finances are in good hands. Finally, when you and your spouse are stuck in different views, a CFP being a neutral 3rd party and an experienced professional may be a big help to you when it comes to clarifying goals and presenting alternatives in which you and your spouse can live with

However, if you have problems trusting strangers to manage your money or you want to avoid huge CFP fees, then you can just opt to approach people you know who are financially literate, or you can simply read up a lot of other books for self-investment and related topics which can help you verify that what other people say are indeed true.

Working Together and Handling Disputes

Working on a goal by investing together as a couple, you are bound to clash along your journey. Before you and your spouse hit the end of the road, develop a method to work out disputes. Always try to be objectives and remove emotional decision-making. Analyze the risks versus rewards, and the costs versus benefits.

If you faces too much disagreements that pooling all your money together would be hard for you as a couple to work with, then having a separate savings account for each of you may be the fallback plan. This allows one party to have his/her own set of significant expenses such as job- or business-related expenses, or other expenses in which the other party is not comfortable to spend their money on. This can include more risky investment that one of you are more keen to take while the other wants to avoid completely. Agree on a certain percentage of your income to be placed in your joint account – where the budget of household expenses will be taken from – and the remaining will then be for the individual's own consumption such as pursuing an interest, covering personal expenses, or personal investment. Periodically review this percentage to see if either party is comfortable to contribute more. If one party's personal investment ends up pretty good, he or she can always choose to cover some additional common expenses from his personal account every now and then, so that the common expense can grow faster, which means both of you can create wealth faster together.

Managing the Investment Together

Making the decision to create wealth together is a long term commitment and a journey that both of you undertake together. So both of you need to be involved in actively managing it, from checking your expenses against your budget, to reviewing your investment performance. Schedule regular time to sit down and talk to your partner about how your plans are going, and decide together whether there is a need to make any adjustments as a result to some changes in your lives over the years. For example, if you got a promotion, could you contribute more to the common investment pool so you have more money every month for investment? If you like to pursue an interest and need to take on more expenses every month, and if you do not have personal account to draw from, could you factor this item into your common budget, and evaluate the impact to your saving and investment plans? These are just some examples, and there could be many more others which could influence your budget, your investments etc.

Make sure to communicate with your spouse often and be open during the discussion, as finances are one of the major causes of separation between couples. The more open you are with your spouse about your finances, the less likely you are to panic when something substantial occurs to you personally or within the markets where you invested in.

Investing together means you have the potential to realize capital gains and receive interest and/or dividends as a team. Deciding to invest together requires commitment to each other because it can be a total nightmare to wind up your mutual investments when your relationship turn sour and both of you need to go separate ways. Thus investing together really is an act that will help to solidify your marriage, and hold you to your promises to each other - **"For Richer or For Poorer"**.

Do remember also, it is the journey and process of doing this together that should be fun, enjoyable and meaningful. Both of you should work towards a common dream or objective so as to create wealth **together**. It is a long journey, do not forget to still allow yourselves to be happy along the way. Enjoy each other's company and have fun along the way of reaching your goals. You definitely do not want to end up creating wealth but both of you are unhappy and thus unable to enjoy the fruits of your labor together.

Chapter 6 - The Pursuit of Wealth

Defining Wealth Creation

We talk a lot in this book about creating wealth. By that, I do not mean creating the wealth of the "filthy rich" like Warren Buffet, Steve Jobs, or Bill Gates. What I like you to aim for is to have more than enough money to cover for what you need, and being financially independent so that you are able to do things that you enjoy together, or work on what you like to work on, without having to constantly worry about money for the rest of your life.

You do not need to have billions of dollars to reach that goal. Even if you have billions, if you do not have the health to enjoy, or if you do not have your loving partner besides you when you get there, then what is the point? Would it not be nicer to have your loved ones always healthy and safe besides you, and all of you are able to enjoy the loving company with each other, while knowing that all your money needs are covered so you need not have to keep worrying about it? So knowing the endpoint is important, and you should recognize that money is just a means to an end, and not an endpoint by itself. If you have enough money to meet those endpoints that are really important to you, you are already wealthy, and the additional pursuit of further wealth may add joy and satisfaction to both of you, but it should not drive you too hard that you need to sacrifice any of your endpoint.

So knowing what wealth creation is really about can help you prioritize and be more effective in making major decisions along your journey. Your end state is to have your loving relationship maintained intact as you build your wealth to the point where you can continue to enjoy each other's company happily, and your partner is safe and healthy, and both of you do not need to worry about money. If you think everything is all about money, then you may end up sacrificing some things along the way without realizing it, and then when you have all those money and start looking back, you may not have the important things beside you. Example, if you argue all the time about which investment to make to optimize your returns, but end up with a soured relationship, even if you get a very high return on investment ultimately, is it worth it ultimately?

Be a Wealthy Couple

As a couple, it is important to know that being rich does not only mean having a lot of money, but it also means that you emotionally feel that you have enough to meet everything you need. And this includes the feeling of being loved by your partner, being happy with each other's company, and knowing that your loved ones are happy as well. If you are not happy with some aspects of your life, then simply doing or buying more of the same things that you already own with the money you have will be of no help. But if you find yourself happy with what you have in life – your spouse, your kids, a house of your own, etc. – then more money is just frosting on a cupcake. It is not really necessary.

Being wealthy is not about more money, but rather about being happy and satisfied with what you can get. Being rich means having enough for you and your spouse to spend to cover what you need and like, including some memorable trips and occasions with your partner so that you continue to build and maintain the intimate relationship with each other.

Observe the typical millionaire couples out there. They do not buy clothes at classy stores or swap cars frequently. Many do not even live in upscale neighborhoods. They rather choose to live in humble houses, because they understand that an expensive house does not make a nice home. They have everything they need, and they do not feel that having fancy dresses will make them feel any more wealthier. They also do not need to show people that they are wealthy because they know that they already are.

The Secret to Growing Wealthy

Once you understand the real meaning of getting wealthy, and have worked out ways to pursue this together without constantly getting into disagreements and fights that derail your journey or stop it completely, you are now ready for the biggest secret to wealth creation.

The secret to wealth creation really is so simple you may think I am fooling you, but I am not. It just involves the following

1. Spend Less Than You Earn and Save Monthly
2. Invest Your Saving for a Reasonable Return Consistently
3. Leverage the Power of Compounding
4. Start Early!

That's it! Simple but effective, though in practice it can be difficult if you are not well prepared. Some of these steps are way too advance for you right now, and are big topics by itself that not a single book can give you all the knowledge you need. So you need to continue to get educated about them - together! We will just cover them briefly below.

Spend Less Than You Earn and Save Monthly

This is briefly covered in earlier chapter where we talk about establishing a common budget and plan. If done correctly, you will end up with a surplus every month, which you can use for investment. The speed of wealth increase depends on how much you can save up every month. By working together and ensuring that you do not keep fighting over disagreements, you can work together to set up a comfortable budget that still allow both of you to enjoy your wealth creation journey together, and to optimize every cent you earn and put them to good use.

You are advised to research more on how to do such budgeting in detail so you have better ideas on how to allocate money and save more, and to spend your money wisely and optimally as a couple. Alternatively, look into ways of earning extra income outside salaries from your jobs too, so as to increase the earnings, which also allow you to save more assuming you do not spend every excess dollars you earn.

Invest Your Saving for a Reasonable Return Consistently

Chapter 4 gives a simple introduction to investment, but this is definitely not sufficient for you. There are tons of books and courses out there that talks about various investment strategies and approaches, as well as various investment instruments. When you are first starting out, I recommend just focus on safe blue-chip shares. As your financial knowledge and experience increases over time, you can start looking at more complex instruments that involve much higher risks, but can compensate you with higher returns. Always remember the risk-return tradeoff - the higher the promised returns, the higher the risks, and diversification is key to allow you to spread your risks.

The higher the return, the faster the wealth creation process, but risk of your investment going sour can increase and when that happens, your plan can be set back significantly. You need not go for returns that brings you double your investments, or even 30-50%. An investment of 5-8% may already be very good if you can consistently achieve this. You can then leverage on the power of compounding to do the rest.

(Note - in times and places of high inflation, this return may need to be higher to compensate for the effects of inflation)

Leverage the Power of Compounding

To really grow wealthy, you need to apply the principle of compounded interest in your investment. For instance, you and your partner agree to invest **$1,000** per month at a compounded interest rate of **5% for 30 years**. By the end of 30 years, when you decide to retire, you will have an amount of **$840,194.12**. And that still excludes the money you have invested in your 401(k). Isn't that exciting? That will indeed be a comfortable figure to enjoy with once you stop working.

Below are a few examples to illustrate the power of compounding, and the various factors that influence it.

- If you invest **$1,201.55** per month at a compounded rate of 5% for 30 years, you will get **$1 million** at the end of the period.

- If you invest **$670.98** per month at a compounded rate of **8% for 30 years**, you will get **$1 million** at the end of the period

- If you can spare **$1,341.96** per month and consistently get **8%** compounded for 30 years, you will get **$2 million** instead of $1 million at the end of the period!

- If you only have **20 years** to invest, assuming you can still get **8%** compounded interest, in order to just get your **$1 million**, you would need to save **$1,697.73** monthly. ie. Almost 3 times what you need if you had started 10 years earlier!

Start Early!

For compounded interest to work its magic, it must have enough time. This is evident from the last example above, where instead of 30 years, if you only have 20 years, then you need to save almost 3 times more every month to hit your $1 million target. Conversely, if you are not able to save so much, then you would just end up with a smaller nest egg at the end of the period.

Which is why for young couples like you who are just starting up, the best time to start is NOW!

Conclusion

Many people have their own definition of wealthy. But whether you are wealthy or not depends on yourself. If you are driven by money, no amount of money may make you wealthy enough. If you view wealthy as being financially abundant so that you have enough to cover for your needs while you and your loved ones are beside you to enjoy life together in a meaningful relationship, then it becomes much more achievable for you to get wealthy.

Once you believe that you can get wealthy, the question becomes how to get there. The secret to getting there is really very simple, and it is outlined in Chapter 6 - The Pursuit of Wealth.

However, even though they seem simple, it is much harder in practice. It will take a lifelong commitment to keep getting educated financially and continuous monitoring of your budgets and plans to make sure they are on track. The journey is full of surprises and obstacles, so the need to constantly monitor and re-plan is critical to ensure that your plan stays relevant, and you are financially prepared for various scenarios that happen along the way.

The whole process of wealth creation is difficult enough for an individual, and if you now have two person that must do it together, it adds another big dimension of complexity and difficulty, because you will likely have differences in opinions and ideas. It is a very sad fact to know that many couples end up separated or divorced after too much disagreements and quarrels over financial matters. The irony is that many couples probably started up wanting to create wealth together, but due to differences along the way that is not handled well, relationship starts to sour and disagreements turn to fights and finally the whole plan is derailed. So this is a very dangerous zone that must be threaded very carefully.

Careful planning and discussions must therefore be done first before you undertake the journey together. You need to spend time understanding each other's money personality, and agree on the rules upfront when fights inevitably occur. There should never be any hit below belts, and any fights should really be a friendly sparring exercise.

Keep in mind always that you are both on the same journey to creating the financial dreams you shared together, and should always work together as a team. There will indeed be dark times along the way of meeting your goals as a couple. It is unavoidable, especially when things do not come out as what you expect them to be. But instances such as these should not keep you from striving harder together. Do not let bad times bring both of you down and discourage you from proceeding with your plans - you just need to re-adjust it. Do not also let disagreements between you end the journey. Focus on enjoying the journey together instead, and you will find that the journey may be much more important than the destination too.

I have come to the end of my book, and I would like to thank you for reading till the last page. I hope to have given you sound advice along the way to get you started on the right track in your journey to creating wealth **together.** Along the journey, there are many more obstacles that you will likely meet, and many more knowledge that you will need to acquire, but I hope you now have the confidence and the initial knowledge to pursue this together, and may you be successful in your journey.

As promised, I am including a zip file which contains some resources which I hope can help you. It includes a simple risk profile questionnaire as well as a simple template for budgeting. By downloading this zip file, you would be put on a mailing list which you can opt out at any time. Through this mailing list, I will from time to time introduce you to various new ideas, products and services which I believe can help you along in your journey and make it easier for you. It is of course up to you to evaluate if they are useful, but no harm receiving extra advices at no cost right?

Finally, may I humbly and sincerely request your help to write a review for this book? Your kindness is much appreciated.

-- Serene Genie

FREE Resource Links

Free Tools

Download the Zip File for Free to get access to

1. Risk Profile Questionnaire

2. Sample Budget Template

URL - http://free-item-for-me.com/create-wealth-zip/

Other Books by Serene Genie

1. **Mindful Meditation, Anyone, Anytime, Anywhere - Achieve a Stress-Free, Healthy and Happy Lifestyle**

2. **Overpowering Depression and Anxiety - The Drug Free and Sustainable Way**

Good Books on Investments

1. **The Intelligent Investor** - Benjamin Graham

2. **The Snowball: Warren Buffet and the Business of Life** - Alice Schroeder

3. **Rich Dad Poor Dad** - Robert Kiyosaki

4. **One Up on Wall Street** - Peter Lynch

www.ingramcontent.com/pod-product-compliance
Lightning Source LLC
Chambersburg PA
CBHW040851180526
45159CB00001B/394